MONSTER SHAKES

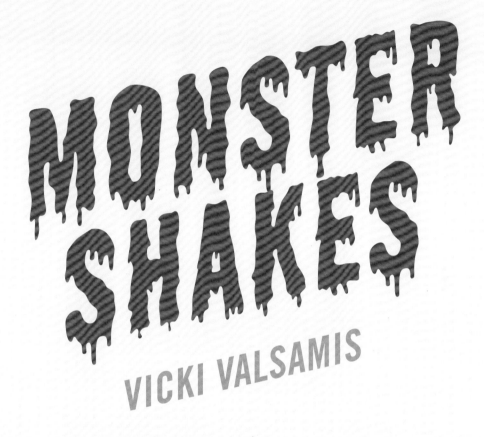

MONSTER SHAKES

VICKI VALSAMIS

Smith
Street
Books

CONTENTS

INTRODUCTION

The secret to the ultimate monster shake is always: more is more. You should see the recipes in this book as starting points – don't be afraid to go a little crazy and pile those toppings on sky-high.

Construction is key when it comes to a fully stacked shake, so here are a few hints and tips to help you on your way.

STABILITY

It's important to start with a good base on top of which to pile ingredients. A scoop of ice cream in the shake will help hold up cream or frosting, and a well-placed donut or cookie on the rim of your glass will give you the solid foundations you need for extreme monstering.

GLASSWARE

I recommend using 500 ml (17 fl oz/2 cup) mason jars for monster shakes. There's plenty of room inside the jar for your shake and the inset, threaded rims help the cream or frosting to stick and allow for a bit of extra support when piling on your toppings. A straight-sided or tapered-out glass may result in the cream or frosting sliding down the edges.

OTHER EQUIPMENT

You generally don't need a lot of gear to make a monster shake, and the essentials are things you probably have in your kitchen cupboards.

Blender: a powerful 'jug' blender is a great piece of kit for making smooth, frothy shakes, but if you don't have one, a hand-held blender or food processor will more than do the trick.

Piping bag: neccessary for piping on cream or frosting and filling donuts. A large star-shaped nozzle and a medium-sized round nozzle should cover most of your bases. These are generally inexpensive, but if you don't have one, you can improvise by snipping the corner off a clean freezer bag or zip lock bag.

Plastic squeeze bottles: not essential but very useful for all of your syrup drizzling needs.

Skewers: you'll need skewers for threading candy, fruit, marshmallows and other toppings, as well as for holding things like cupcakes in place. Looks are very important to a monster shake so don't feel restricted by standard bamboo skewers – find some colourful plastic swizzle sticks or decorative toothpicks for extra fun.

DAIRY FREE

I don't want anyone to miss out, so we've included a few dairy-free options, marked 'DF'. In all cases the shake doesn't contain dairy, but you may need to tweak your toppings to suit.

EATING

I don't want to tell you how to devour your monstrous masterpiece, but certainly a straw and a long spoon will get you started. If your shake is topped with a donut, cookie or brownie, try dunking it into the liquid. And if your shake is topped with wafer rolls, try sucking the shake through like a straw for an extra flavour hit.

SKY-HIGH BLUEBERRY WAFFLE STACK

SHAKE

500 ml (17 fl oz/2 cups)
  milk
310 g (11 oz/2 cups) fresh
  or frozen blueberries
1 tablespoon vanilla extract
2 tablespoons maple syrup
1 scoop vanilla ice cream

MONSTER YOUR SHAKE

Buttercream frosting
  (page 124)
2 scoops vanilla ice cream
Whipped cream (page 122)
2 Blueberry waffles
  (page 129), cut into
  quarters
fresh blueberries, for
  decorating

SERVES 2

Breakfast or dessert? Why should you have to choose? This shake is a tower built in celebration of both and does not disappoint on either count.

To make the shake, combine the ingredients in a blender or food processor. Blend until smooth and combined.

Using a spatula, smear the frosting around the outer rims of the glasses. Gently pour in the shake (reserve a small amount for drizzling) and top with a scoop of ice cream.

Using a piping bag fitted with a star nozzle, pipe a generous amount of whipped cream on top of the shakes. Gently place the waffle pieces into the cream, adding more cream as required. Top with the blueberries and drizzle with the reserved shake.

RASPBERRY BERET

SHAKE

250 ml (8½ fl oz/1 cup) milk
125 g (4½ oz/1 cup) fresh
   or frozen raspberries
2 tablespoons Raspberry
   syrup (page 121)
1 scoop raspberry sorbet

MONSTER YOUR SHAKE

85 g (3 oz) packet
   raspberry jelly crystals
Whipped cream (page 122)
2 scoops vanilla ice cream
4 marshmallow cookies
   (such as Iced Vovos)
red sprinkles, for
   decorating
fresh raspberries,
   for decorating
raspberry gummies,
   for decorating
edible flowers, for
   decorating

SERVES 2

A layer of raspberry jelly set at a jaunty angle serves as the perfect base for this fruity treat.

Mix the jelly according to the packet instructions. Divide the mixture between the glasses and place in the fridge, leaning securely against a bowl so the glasses sit at an angle. Chill for at least 2 hours or until set.

To make the shake, combine the ingredients in a blender or food processor. Blend until smooth and combined.

Using a spatula, smear some whipped cream around the outer rims of the glasses. Gently pour in the shake and top with a scoop of ice cream.

Using a piping bag fitted with a star nozzle, pipe a generous amount of whipped cream onto the top of the shakes. Slide in two marshmallow cookies each, pipe on a little more cream and decorate with the sprinkles, fresh raspberries, raspberry gummies and flowers.

STRAWBERRY ROLLER-COASTER DONUT APOCALYPSE

SHAKE

500 ml (17 fl oz/2 cups)
    milk
300 g (10½ oz) fresh or
    frozen strawberries
90 g (3 oz/⅓ cup)
    Buttercream frosting
    (page 124)
2 scoops strawberry
    ice cream

MONSTER YOUR SHAKE

125 ml (4 fl oz/½ cup)
    Strawberry syrup
    (page 121)
Buttercream frosting,
    coloured pink (page 124)
20 strawberry chocolate
    candies
2 scoops strawberry
    ice cream
2 Jelly/jam-filled donuts
    (page 132)
2 strawberry chocolate
    lollipops
pink cotton candy,
    for decorating
2 large strawberries,
    cut in half

SERVES 2

Strawberry heaven crossed with a day at an amusement park – with all of the cotton candy and jelly donuts you could dream of.

To make the shake, combine the ingredients in a blender or food processor. Blend until smooth and combined.

Line the inside of each glass with strawberry syrup. Using a piping bag fitted with a star nozzle, pipe the frosting around the outer rims, then decorate with the strawberry chocolate candies. Gently pour in the shake and top with a scoop ice cream.

Top each glass with a donut. Gently stick in the lollipops and decorate with fairy floss and the strawberry halves.

MAPLE—BACON FRENCH TOAST BANANAPALOOZA

SHAKE

500 ml (17 fl oz/2 cups) milk
240 g (8½ oz/1 cup) mashed banana
1 teaspoon ground cinnamon
125 ml (4 fl oz/½ cup) Caramel syrup (page 120)
2 scoops vanilla ice cream

MONSTER YOUR SHAKE

Buttercream frosting (page 124)
1 small banana, sliced
2 scoops vanilla ice cream
Candied bacon (page 128)
Whipped cream (page 122)
French toast (page 128)
maple syrup, for drizzling
Caramel syrup (page 120)

SERVES 2

An epic breakfast in shake form. Stack up your candied bacon, banana and French toast and then slather it all in maple syrup.

To make the shake, combine the ingredients in a blender or food processor. Blend until smooth and combined.

Using a spatula, smear the frosting around the outer rim of each glass then decorate with the sliced banana. Gently pour in the shake and top with a scoop of ice cream.

Place a slice of candied bacon on top of each glass. Using a piping bag fitted with a star nozzle, pipe a generous amount of whipped cream on top of the shakes. Top with a piece of French toast and the remaining bacon. Drizzle with maple syrup and caramel syrup.

MANGO–PASSIONFRUIT MANIC MERINGUE

SHAKE

375 ml (12½ fl oz/1½ cups) milk
315 g (11 oz) chopped fresh or frozen mango
juice of ½ lime
4 scoops mango sorbet
90 g (3 oz/⅓ cup) passionfruit pulp

MONSTER YOUR SHAKE

Passionfruit curd (page 126)
½ mango, flesh thinly sliced
2 Cinnamon donuts (page 132)
Italian meringue topping (page 123)
1 passionfruit, cut into quarters
fresh blueberries, for decorating
1 round caramel wafer, cut in half

SERVES 2

This is like a sweet tropical storm, with oozing passionfruit curd and a silky meringue topping.

To make the shake, combine the milk, mango, lime juice and sorbet in a blender or food processor. Blend until smooth and combined, then stir in the passionfruit pulp.

Using a spatula, smear the passionfruit curd around the outer rim of each glass and gently pour in the shake.

Thread half the mango slices onto two skewers. Top each shake with a cinnamon donut and stick the skewers in.

Using a piping bag fitted with a medium round nozzle, pipe a small mound of meringue in the middle of each donut. Lightly brown the meringue using a kitchen blowtorch.

Nestle the passionfruit quarters into the meringue and top with the blueberries, wafer halves and remaining mango slices.

LIME COCO-LOCO COCONUT

SHAKE

625 ml (21 fl oz/2½ cups)
  unsweetened almond
  or soy milk
250 g (9 oz/1 cup) coconut
  cream
1 tablespoon fresh lime
  juice
1 tablespoon coconut
  essence
60 ml (2 fl oz/¼ cup) agave
  nectar
100 g (3½ oz) frozen
  coconut flesh

MONSTER YOUR SHAKE

30 g (1 oz/½ cup) coconut
  flakes
Whipped coconut cream
  (page 123)
2 fresh pineapple wedges
4 Coconut cream-filled
  donuts (page 132)
1 lime, sliced or quartered
pineapple leaves, for
  decorating
1 teaspoon lime zest

SERVES 2

A dairy-free lime and coconut creation that will have you day-dreaming of sunshine and colourful beach umbrellas.

Lightly toast the coconut flakes in a small saucepan over low heat for 2 minutes or until lightly browned. Set aside.

To make the shake, combine the ingredients in a blender or food processor. Blend until smooth and combined.

Using a spatula, smear the outer rim of each glass with some of the whipped coconut cream, then sprinkle with half of the toasted coconut flakes. Gently pour in the shake.

Cut a small slit in the pointy end of each pineapple wedge, then slide onto the rims of the glasses. Using a spoon, heap the remaining coconut cream onto each shake and top with two donuts, the lime wedges and pineapple leaves. Sprinkle with lime zest.

DF

ORANGE SHERBET SPOOKTACULAR

SHAKE

250 ml (8½ fl oz/1 cup) milk
80 g (2¾ oz/¼ cup)
  Orange curd (page 126)
500 ml (17 fl oz/2 cups)
  orange juice
1 tablespoon orange zest
1 tablespoon icing
  (confectioners') sugar
4 scoops vanilla ice cream

MONSTER YOUR SHAKE

White chocolate ganache
  (page 125)
orange sprinkles, for
  decorating
2 scoops vanilla ice cream
Orange blossom whipped
  cream (page 122)
Choc-dipped oranges
  (page 126)
1 ice cream wafer, cut in
  half on an angle
2 choc-orange cookies
orange cotton candy,
  for decorating
1 tablespoon orange zest

SERVES 2

Like the ultimate big tall glass of orange-cream soda-pop.

To make the shake, combine the ingredients in a blender or food processor. Blend until smooth and combined.

Using a spatula, smear the ganache around the outer rim of each glass then decorate with the orange sprinkles. Gently pour in the shake and top with a scoop of ice cream.

Using a piping bag fitted with a star nozzle, pipe a generous amount of whipped cream on top of the shakes. Decorate with the choc-dipped oranges, wafer halves, cookies and cotton candy, and sprinkle with zest.

TROPICAL POPSICLE HURRICANE

SHAKE

650 ml (22 fl oz) pineapple
  juice
100 ml (3½ fl oz) lychee
  syrup
80 g (2¾ oz/¼ cup) Lime
  curd (page 126)
juice and zest of 2 limes
4 scoops pineapple,
  coconut or lime sorbet

MONSTER YOUR SHAKE

4 lychees
4 cubes fresh pineapple
Whipped coconut cream
  (page 123)
1 tablespoon lime zest
2 scoops pineapple,
  coconut or lime sorbet
2 watermelon wedges
1 lime, sliced or cut into
  wedges
2 pine–lime popsicles
dried blueberries, for
  decorating

SERVES 2

Lime, lychee, pineapple and watermelon topped with an ice-cold popsicle. It's a maelstrom of sweet summery goodness.

To make the shake, combine the ingredients in a blender or food processor. Blend until smooth and combined.

Thread the lychees and pineapple cubes onto two skewers.

Using a spatula, smear some of the whipped coconut cream around the outer rim of each glass, then sprinkle with the lime zest. Gently pour in the shake and top with a scoop of sorbet.

Cut a small slit in the pointy end of each watermelon wedge, then slide onto the rims of the glasses.

Spoon more coconut cream on top of the shakes and top with the fruit skewers and lime. Insert the popsicle so it sits upside-down and sprinkle with the blueberries.

DF

BANANARAMA GRANOLA CRUSH

SHAKE

400 ml (13½ fl oz) soy milk
150 ml (5 fl oz) coconut milk
1 small avocado
240 g (8½ oz/1 cup) mashed banana
2 sprigs mint, leaves picked
1 teaspoon vanilla bean paste
90 g (3 oz/¼ cup) honey
1 tablespoon chia seeds
2 scoops vanilla soy ice cream

MONSTER YOUR SHAKE

30 g (1 oz/½ cup) coconut flakes
3 crunchy oat and honey granola bars
Whipped coconut cream (page 123)
2 scoops vanilla soy ice cream
1 banana, thickly sliced
maple syrup, for drizzling

SERVES 2

A healthy breakfast hidden in a monster shake. Is this Dr Jekyll or Mr Hyde? Who knows – all that matters is that it's delicious.

Lightly toast the coconut flakes in a small saucepan over low heat for 2 minutes or until lightly browned. Set aside.

To make the shake, combine the ingredients in a blender or food processor. Blend until smooth and combined.

Place one of the granola bars in a zip lock bag and crush with a rolling pin or wooden spoon.

Using a spatula, smear some of the whipped coconut cream around the outer rim of each glass, then decorate with the crushed granola bar. Gently pour in the shake and top with a scoop of ice cream.

Cut a small slit in two of the banana slices, then slide onto the rims of the glasses.

Place a granola bar across the top of each glass, and top with more whipped coconut cream. Decorate with the remaining banana slices and coconut flakes and drizzle with maple syrup.

DF

PEACHES & CREAM MARSHMALLOW DREAM

SHAKE

375 ml (12½ fl oz/1½ cups)
 milk
200 g (7 oz/1 cup) drained
 tinned peach slices
125 ml (4 fl oz/½ cup)
 peach syrup
185 ml (6 fl oz/¾ cup)
 thickened cream
2 scoops vanilla ice cream

MONSTER YOUR SHAKE

Buttercream frosting
 (page 124)
2 scoops peach or vanilla
 ice cream
2 Cinnamon donuts
 (page 132)
Whipped cream (page 122)
6 dried peach halves
4 vanilla wafer rolls
2 marshmallows
Caramel syrup (page 120)

SERVES 2

Luscious peaches and cream – the perfect partners in crime for a shake that is just pretending to be oh-so sweet and innocent.

To make the shake, combine the ingredients in a blender or food processor. Blend until smooth and combined.

Using a spatula, smear the frosting around the outer rim of each glass. Gently pour in the shake and top with a scoop of ice cream.

Cut a small slit in the side of each donut, then slide onto the rims of the glasses.

Using a piping bag fitted with a star nozzle, pipe a generous amount of whipped cream on top of the shakes. Top with the dried peaches, wafer rolls and marshmallows. Lightly brown the marshmallows using a kitchen blowtorch, then drizzle everything with caramel syrup.

KILLER VANILLA

SHAKE

625 ml (21 fl oz/2½ cups)
  milk
2 tablespoons vanilla bean
  paste
60 ml (2 fl oz/¼ cup) vanilla
  syrup
3 scoops vanilla ice cream

MONSTER YOUR SHAKE

White chocolate ganache
  (page 125)
2 scoops vanilla ice cream
Vanilla bean whipped
  cream (page 122)
1 White choc-chip waffle
  (page 129), cut in half
4 vanilla wafer rolls
mint leaves, for decorating
vanilla cotton candy, for
  decorating

SERVES 2

Oozing with white chocolate ganache and finished with waffles – there's nothing 'plain' about this vanilla monster.

To make the shake, combine the ingredients in a blender or food processor. Blend until smooth and combined.

Line the inside and the outer rim of each glass with white chocolate ganache. Gently pour in the shake and top with a scoop of ice cream.

Pile the whipped cream on top of the shakes and top each with a waffle. Decorate with the wafer rolls, mint leaves and cotton candy.

ANNIHILATION BY CHOCOLATE

SHAKE

500 ml (17 fl oz/2 cups)
  milk
125 ml (4 fl oz/½ cup)
  Chocolate syrup
  (page 120)
5 scoops chocolate-chip
  ice cream

MONSTER YOUR SHAKE

Chocolate syrup (page 120)
155 g (5½ oz/½ cup) Nutella
chocolate sprinkles,
  for decorating
2 scoops chocolate-chip
  ice cream
Whipped cream (page 122)
2 Choc-chip waffles
  (page 129)
2 chocolate wafer rolls
2 Nutella-filled donuts
  (page 132)
2 chocolate-coated
  chocolate cookies
  (such as TimTams)
chocolate cotton candy,
  for decorating
2 Mini chocolate-
  topped cupcakes
  (page 131)

SERVES 2

There's 'death by chocolate' and then there's this: complete and utter, one hundred per cent total annihilation by chocolate.

To make the shake, combine the ingredients in a blender or food processor. Blend until smooth and combined.

Line the inside of each glass with syrup. Smear the Nutella around the outer rims, then decorate with the sprinkles. Gently pour in the shake and top with a scoop of ice cream.

Using a piping bag fitted with a star nozzle, top the shakes with some whipped cream and then cover with the waffles. Poke the wafer rolls through the waffle then, piping blobs of cream where necessary to help things stick, top with the donuts, cookies, cotton candy and cupcakes.

STRAWBERRY SUCKER-PUNCH

SHAKE

375 ml (12½ fl oz/1½ cups)
milk
125 ml (4 fl oz/½ cup)
Strawberry syrup
(page 121)
300 g (10½ oz) fresh or
frozen strawberries
4 scoops strawberry
ice cream

MONSTER YOUR SHAKE

150 g (5½ oz/1 cup) white
chocolate buttons
75 g (2¾ oz) fresh
strawberries, plus extra
for garnish
red sprinkles, for decorating
Strawberry syrup (page 121)
4 scoops strawberry ice
cream
Whipped cream (page 122)
2 ice cream wafer cones
1 toasted strawberry
Pop-Tart, cut in half
2 strawberry Oreo cookies
4 strawberry Pocky sticks

SERVES 2

When too much strawberry just isn't enough.

Place the chocolate buttons in a heatproof bowl set over a saucepan of gently simmering water, making sure the base of the bowl doesn't touch the water. Stir occasionally until melted and smooth. Dip the strawberries into the chocolate and place on a baking paper-lined tray to set. Keep the remaining chocolate warm.

To make the shake, combine the ingredients in a blender or food processor. Blend until smooth and combined.

Dip the rims of the glasses into the remaining melted chocolate and decorate with the red sprinkles. Line the insides with strawberry syrup, reserving some for topping. Gently pour in the shake and top with a scoop of ice cream. Using a piping bag fitted with a star nozzle, pipe a generous amount of whipped cream on top of the shakes and around the rim of the glasses.

Stick a wafer cone and Pop-Tart into each shake. Fill the cones with the remaining ice cream and the choc-dipped strawberries, some whipped cream and the Oreos. Decorate with the Pocky sticks and extra strawberries, then drizzle with the reserved syrup.

WICKED SALTED CARAMEL

SHAKE

500 ml (17 fl oz/2 cups)
 milk
125 ml (4 fl oz/½ cup)
 Salted caramel syrup
 (page 120)
3 scoops butterscotch
 ice cream

MONSTER YOUR SHAKE

Salted caramel syrup
 (page 120)
Whipped cream (page 122)
50 g (½ cup) walnut halves,
 roughly chopped
1 Snickers Bar, roughly
 chopped
2 Choc-chip waffles
 (page 129), cut into long
 pieces
6 pretzel sticks
icing (confectioners') sugar,
 for dusting

SERVES 2

When salty and sweet combine their considerable forces, something truly magical happens. Case in point.

To make the shake, combine the ingredients in a blender or food processor. Blend until smooth and combined.

Line the outside of each glass with syrup. Using a piping bag fitted with a star nozzle, pipe a generous amount of whipped cream around the rim of each glass, then decorate with some of the crushed walnuts and chopped Snickers Bar. Gently pour in the shake.

Stick the waffle pieces into the shakes, piping more whipped cream in to keep them in place. Decorate with remaining walnuts and Snickers Bar, and the pretzel sticks. Dust with icing sugar and drizzle with more caramel syrup.

I SCREAM FOR COOKIES & CREAM

SHAKE

500 ml (17 fl oz/2 cups)
  milk
125 ml (4 fl oz/½ cup)
  Chocolate syrup
  (page 120)
4 scoops cookies-and-
  cream ice cream

MONSTER YOUR SHAKE

Chocolate Ganache
  (page 125)
4 scoops cookies-and-
  cream ice cream
Whipped cream (page 122)
2 Chocolate-frosted donuts
  (page 132)
1 cookies-and-cream
  chocolate bar, cut in half
6 cookies-and-cream
  Pocky sticks
2 ice cream wafers
1 chocolate cookie,
  crushed

SERVES 2

A classic diner treat monster-fied with chocolate donuts for your dunking pleasure!

To make the shake, combine the ingredients in a blender or food processor. Blend until smooth and combined.

Dip the rims of the glasses into the chocolate ganache, reserving the remainder for topping, and sit upright, allowing the ganache to drizzle down the glasses. Gently pour in the shake and top with a scoop of ice cream.

Using a piping bag fitted with a star nozzle, pipe whipped cream over the shakes and around the rim of each glass. Top with the donuts, chocolate bar pieces, Pocky sticks, remaining ice cream and the wafers. Sprinkle with the crushed cookie and drizzle with the remaining ganache.

CRAZY CARAMEL CAPPUCCINO

SHAKE

500 ml (17 fl oz/2 cups)
  milk
2 tablespoons instant
  coffee granules
2 tablespoons icing
  (confectioners') sugar
4 scoops vanilla or coffee
  ice cream

MONSTER YOUR SHAKE

Mocha buttercream
  frosting (page 124)
10 choc-coated almonds,
  5 roughly chopped
2 scoops vanilla or coffee
  ice cream
Whipped cream (page 122)
2 Cinnamon donuts
  (page 132)
3 chocolate wafer rolls,
  2 whole and 1 cut in half
cocoa powder, for dusting
60 ml (3 fl oz/¼ cup)
  Caramel syrup (page 120)

SERVES 2

Rich and full-flavoured with lots of froth. Try sucking the shake up through the chocolate wafer rolls for an intense flavour hit.

To make the shake, combine the ingredients in a blender or food processor. Blend until smooth and very frothy.

Using a spatula, smear the frosting around the outer rim of each glass, then decorate with some of the chopped almonds. Gently pour in the shake and top with a scoop of ice cream.

Using a piping bag fitted with a star nozzle, pipe a generous amount of whipped cream on top of the shakes. Top with the donuts, wafer rolls, more whipped cream and the remaining almonds. Dust with cocoa powder and drizzle with caramel syrup.

CHAI NOUGAT BONANZA

SHAKE

750 ml (25½ fl oz/3 cups)
   unsweetened almond or
   soy milk
1 teaspoon ground
   cinnamon
½ teaspoon ground
   nutmeg
1 teaspoon vanilla bean
   paste
¼ teaspoon ground cloves
¼ teaspoon ground
   cardamom
¼ teaspoon ground ginger
4 pitted dates
90 g (3 oz/¼ cup) honey
2 scoops vanilla soy
   ice cream

MONSTER YOUR SHAKE

175 g (6 oz/½ cup) honey
Whipped coconut cream
   (page 123)
2 ice cream wafers, cut
   into wedges
1 slice soft Italian nougat
   cake, roughly broken
   into chunks
ground cinnamon,
   for dusting

SERVES 2

Soaking the donuts in the shake and devouring with a spoon is pure monster magic. For an extra flavour punch, try doubling the spices.

To make the shake, combine the ingredients in a blender or food processor. Blend until smooth and combined.

Line the inside of each glass with half the honey. Gently pour in the shake.

Using a piping bag fitted with a star nozzle, pipe a generous amount of whipped coconut cream on top of the shakes. Stick the wafers in and top with pieces of nougat cake, alternating with more whipped coconut cream. Dust with cinnamon and drizzle with the remaining honey.

DF

CHOC-MINT ICE-CREAM SANDWICH MELTDOWN

SHAKE

625 ml (21 fl oz/2½ cups) milk
60 ml (2 fl oz/¼ cup) Chocolate syrup (page 120)
½ teaspoon peppermint extract
10 drops green food colouring
3 scoops peppermint choc-chip ice cream

MONSTER YOUR SHAKE

4 scoops peppermint choc-chip ice cream
4 large chocolate cookies
125 ml (4 fl oz/½ cup) Chocolate syrup (page 120)
Choc-mint buttercream frosting (page 124)
1 crunchy peppermint chocolate bar (such as Peppermint Crisp), crushed
Peppermint whipped cream (page 122)
1 mint Kit Kat, broken into sticks

SERVES 2

What a dynamic duo these two make! This super smooth shake blend has a refreshing minty flavour, and it satisfies those chocolate cravings all in one monstrous hit.

Place a scoop of ice cream onto two of the cookies. Top with the remaining cookies and press together to create ice-cream sandwiches. Place in the freezer until ready to use.

To make the shake, combine the ingredients in a blender or food processor. Blend until smooth and combined.

Line the inside of each glass with syrup. Smear the frosting around the outer rims, then sprinkle with the crushed peppermint chocolate bar. Gently pour in the shake and top with the remaining scoops of ice cream.

Place an ice cream sandwich onto each glass and, using a piping bag fitted with a star nozzle, pipe whipped cream into the gaps, creating a slight mound at the front. Decorate with the Kit Kat sticks.

BRANDYSNAP MATCHA MADNESS

SHAKE

1 tablespoon matcha
  (green tea powder)
750 ml (25½ fl oz/3 cups)
  soy or unsweetened
  almond milk
1 tablespoon honey
4 scoops vanilla soy ice
  cream

MONSTER YOUR SHAKE

175 g (6 oz/½ cup) honey
4 scoops vanilla soy
  ice cream
Whipped coconut cream
  (page 123)
2 brandysnap baskets
green cotton candy,
  for decorating
2 small pieces fresh
  honeycomb
4 macarons
½ teaspoon black
  sesame seeds

SERVES 2

Your friends will be green-eyed over this green-tea monster!

To make the shake, stir the matcha into 125 ml (4 fl oz/½ cup) warm water, then place in the fridge and cool completely. Combine with the remaining ingredients in a blender or food processor. Blend until smooth and combined.

Line the inside of each glass using most of the honey. Gently pour in the shake and top with a scoop of ice cream. Using a piping bag fitted with a star nozzle, pipe a generous amount of whipped coconut cream on top of the shakes and around the outer rims of the glasses.

Place a brandysnap basket on top of each shake and fill with the remaining ice cream and the cotton candy, honeycomb and macarons. Drizzle with the remaining honey and sprinkle with black sesame seeds.

DF

CHOC-ORANGE BROWNIE JAWBREAKER

SHAKE

500 ml (17 fl oz/2 cups) milk
125 ml (4 fl oz/½ cup) Chocolate syrup (page 120)
2 tablespoons Orange curd (page 126)
zest and juice of 1 large orange
5 scoops chocolate ice cream

MONSTER YOUR SHAKE

Chocolate buttercream frosting (page 124)
orange sprinkles, for decorating
2 scoops chocolate ice cream
Orange blossom whipped cream (page 122)
2 Chocolate brownies (page 130)
6 choc-orange balls (such as Jaffas), 3 crushed
2 choc-orange cookies (such as Jaffa Cakes)
4 choc-orange wafer rolls

SERVES 2

The true secret to this shake is the orange zest, providing an intense orange zing that can't be beat.

To make the shake, combine the ingredients in a blender or food processor. Blend until smooth and combined.

Using a spatula, smear the frosting around the outer rim of each glass then decorate with half the orange sprinkles. Gently pour in the shake and top with a scoop of ice cream.

Using a piping bag fitted with a star nozzle, pipe a generous amount of whipped cream on top of the shakes. Place a brownie across the top of each glass. Top with more whipped cream and decorate with the choc-orange balls, cookies and wafer rolls.

COTTON CANDY DELIRIUM

SHAKE

750 ml (25½ fl oz/3 cups) milk
60 g (2 oz) cotton candy
4 scoops bubblegum ice cream
3 drops red food colouring

MONSTER YOUR SHAKE

150 g (5½ oz/1 cup) milk chocolate buttons
pink and white sprinkles, for decorating
2 scoops bubblegum ice cream
2 Frosted donuts, coloured pink (page 132)
2 ice cream waffle cones
60 g (2 oz) cotton candy
Whipped cream (page 122)
purple and pink mini musk candies, for decorating
4 sprinkle-covered cookies
rainbow sprinkles, for decorating

SERVES 2

Pink overload! Fluffy cotton candy and rainbow sprinkles make for a candy delight.

Place the chocolate buttons in a heatproof bowl set over a saucepan of gently simmering water, making sure the base of the bowl doesn't touch the water. Stir occasionally until melted and smooth. Dip the rims of the glasses into the melted chocolate and sit upright, allowing the chocolate to drizzle down the glasses. Decorate with the pink and white sprinkles.

To make the shake, combine the ingredients in a blender or food processor. Blend until smooth and combined.

Gently pour the shake into the glasses and top with a scoop of ice cream. Place the donuts on top of each glass and set the waffle cone into the hole. Fill the cone with cotton candy and decorate the donut with the mini musk candies.

Using a piping bag fitted with a star nozzle, pipe two blobs of whipped cream on top of each donut. Stick two cookies into the cream and decorate with rainbow sprinkles.

POPPING CANDY BLUE LAGOON

SHAKE

625 ml (21 fl oz/2½ cups) milk
60 ml (2 fl oz/¼ cup) blue raspberry (blue heaven) syrup
4 scoops vanilla ice cream

MONSTER YOUR SHAKE

60 ml (2 fl oz/¼ cup) blue raspberry (blue heaven) syrup
Whipped cream, coloured blue (page 122)
fizzy candy blocks, for decorating
3 tablespoons popping candy
2 Frosted donuts, coloured green (page 132)
4 sherbet cones
2 sour straps

SERVES 2

A crazy blue milkshake that pops and crackles in your mouth? Hell yes!

To make the shake, combine the ingredients in a blender or food processor. Blend until smooth and combined.

Line the inside of each glass with syrup. Using a spatula, smear some of the whipped cream around the outer rims, then decorate with the fizzy candy blocks and some of the popping candy. Gently pour in the shake.

Place the donuts on top and, using a piping bag fitted with a star nozzle, pipe a little whipped cream into the hole. Fill with popping candy. Decorate with the sherbet cones and sour straps.

I HEART CANDY HEARTS

SHAKE

750 ml (25½ fl oz/3 cups)
  milk
60 ml (2 fl oz/¼ cup)
  Strawberry syrup
  (page 121)
60 g (2 oz) cotton candy
4 scoops vanilla ice cream

MONSTER YOUR SHAKE

Strawberry syrup (page 121)
Buttercream frosting,
  coloured pink (page 124)
20 candy hearts
12 marshmallows hearts
4 scoops strawberry ice
  cream
2 mini ice cream cones
Whipped cream (page 122)
2 vanilla wafer rolls
4 chocolate hearts
2 chocolate lollipops
red heart sprinkles,
  for decorating
strawberry chocolate
  drops, for decorating
rainbow sprinkles,
  for decorating

SERVES 2

What says love better than swirls of strawberry topped with sweet candy hearts and puffy marshmallows? You'd be crazy not to say 'I do' to this monster.

To make the shake, combine the ingredients in a blender or food processor. Blend until smooth and combined.

Line the inside of each glass with the strawberry syrup. Using a spatula, smear the frosting around the outer rims, then decorate with the candy and marshmallow hearts. Gently pour in the shake and top with a scoop of ice cream.

Place the remaining scoops of ice cream in the cones and pipe a dollop of cream on top. Stick into the shake along with the wafer rolls, chocolate hearts and lollipops. Decorate with the sprinkles and chocolate drops.

BUTTERSCOTCH POPCORN MIDNIGHT MARATHON

SHAKE

500 ml (17 fl oz/2 cups) milk
125 ml (4 fl oz/½ cup)
  Caramel syrup (page 120)
4 scoops butterscotch ice
  cream

MONSTER YOUR SHAKE

Butterscotch popcorn
  (page 127)
4 large marshmallows,
  halved
Whipped cream (page 122)
2 scoops butterscotch ice
  cream
4 chocolate wafer rolls

SERVES 2

Covered in gooey butterscotch popcorn, this shake is just the thing for an all-night monster-movie marathon.

Make the butterscotch popcorn, but reserve a good amount of the sauce for drizzling. Place the marshmallows on a baking tray and brown the tops using a kitchen blowtorch.

To make the shake, combine the ingredients in a blender or food processor. Blend until smooth and combined.

Line the inside of each glass with some of the reserved butterscotch sauce. Using a spatula, smear some of the whipped cream around the outer rims, then decorate with the marshmallows. Gently pour in the shake and top with a scoop of ice cream.

Cover with more whipped cream then top with mounds of butterscotch popcorn. Stick the wafer rolls in, then drizzle with the remaining butterscotch sauce.

TURKISH DELIGHT EXTRAVAGANZA

SHAKE

4 x 55 g (2 oz) choc-coated
 Turkish delight bars
625 ml (21 fl oz/2½ cups)
 milk
1 tablespoon rosewater
 essence
4 scoops vanilla ice cream
2 drops red food colouring

MONSTER YOUR SHAKE

2 scoops vanilla ice cream
2 x 55 g (2 oz) choc-coated
 Turkish delight bars
Rose whipped cream,
 coloured pink (page 122)
rose cotton candy,
 for decorating
mini musk candies,
 for decorating
pink pearl dust, for
 decorating

SERVES 2

This Turkish delight-infused, thick and gooey mixture is liquid gold – it's just like dringing a chocolate bar.

To make the shake, place the Turkish delight bars and 100 ml (3½ fl oz) of the milk in a saucepan over low heat and stir continuously for 5 minutes or until the Turkish delight is soft. Remove from the heat and use a potato masher to break up into small pieces. Add the remaining milk and place in the fridge to chill. Combine the chilled milk mix with the remaining ingredients in a blender or food processor. Blend until smooth and combined.

Pour the shake into glasses and top with a scoop of ice cream. Place a Turkish delight bar across the top of each glass.

Using a piping bag fitted with a medium-sized round nozzle, pipe a swirl of cream on top of the shake. Decorate with the cotton candy, musk candies and pearl dust.

PEANUT BUTTER PRETZEL CARNAGE

SHAKE

625 ml (21 fl oz/2½ cups) milk
2 tablespoons smooth peanut butter
6 Reese's Peanut Butter Cup Minis, roughly chopped
60 ml (2 fl oz/¼ cup) sweetened condensed milk
4 scoops vanilla ice cream

MONSTER YOUR SHAKE

75 g (2¾ oz/½ cup) dark chocolate buttons
10 pretzels
Chocolate syrup (page 120)
250 g (9 oz/1 cup) smooth peanut butter
Whipped cream (page 122)
2 Choc-chip waffles (page 129), cut in half
2 Reese's Peanut Butter Cups, cut in half
4 Reese's Peanut Butter Cup Minis, 2 cut in half
1 tablespoon crushed peanuts

SERVES 2

Peanut butter fiends! This ultra nutty shake is over the top in the best kind of way.

Place the chocolate buttons in a heatproof bowl set over a saucepan of gently simmering water, making sure the base of the bowl doesn't touch the water. Stir occasionally until melted and smooth. Dip the pretzels halfway into the chocolate and place on a baking paper-lined tray to set.

To make the shake, combine the ingredients in a blender or food processor. Blend until smooth and combined.

Line the inside of each glass with some of the chocolate syrup. Smear the peanut butter around the outer rims, then decorate with most of the pretzels. Gently pour in the shake.

Using a piping bag fitted with a star nozzle, pipe a generous amount of whipped cream on top of the shakes. Carefully stick in the waffle halves to create a 'V' shape, piping more cream in between to help them stick.

Decorate with the Peanut Butter Cups, drizzle with the remaining chocolate syrup and sprinkle with crushed peanuts.

LICKITY-SPLIT LICORICE

SHAKE

180 g (6½ oz) soft choc-
    coated licorice
750 ml (25½ fl oz/3 cups)
    milk
2 scoops licorice or vanilla
    ice cream

MONSTER YOUR SHAKE

2 candy twists (such as
    Twizzlers)
8 licorice allsorts
Whipped cream (page 122)
    6 choc-licorice candies,
    sliced
2 large licorice lollipops

SERVES 2

Infused with soft licorice and topped with sweet licorice candies, you can't get more licorice-y than this!

To make the shake, place the licorice and 100 ml (3½ fl oz) of the milk in a saucepan over low heat and stir continuously for 5 minutes or until the licorice is soft. Remove from the heat and use a potato masher to break up into small pieces. Set aside to cool for 15 minutes. Transfer to a blender or food processor and blend until smooth. Add the remaining milk and place in the fridge to chill. Add the ice cream and blend until smooth and combined.

Meanwhile, tie the candy twists into knots and thread onto two skewers along with the allsorts.

Using a spatula, smear some of the whipped cream around the outer rim of each glass, then decorate with the choc-licorice candies. Gently pour in the shake.

Spoon more whipped cream on top of the shakes and decorate with the lollipops and licorice skewers.

BUBBLEGUM BLOW-OUT

SHAKE

750 ml (25½ fl oz/3 cups)
 milk
200 ml (7 fl oz) bubblegum
 syrup
6 scoops bubblegum
 ice cream

MONSTER YOUR SHAKE

6 pink and white
 marshmallows
125 ml (4 fl oz/½ cup)
 glucose syrup
2 drops purple food
 colouring
Whipped cream (page 122)
blue and pink sprinkles,
 for decorating
4 scoops bubblegum
 ice cream
rocky road, cut into large
 chunks
bubblegum balls,
 for decorating

SERVES 2

A bubblicious shake for stirring up trouble.

To make the shake, combine the ingredients in a blender or food processor. Blend until smooth and combined.

Thread three marshmallows onto the ends of two skewers. In a small bowl, combine the glucose syrup with the food colouring.

Line the inside of each glass with the purple syrup. Using a spatula, smear some of the whipped cream around the outer rims, then decorate with the blue and pink sprinkles. Gently pour in the shake and top with a scoop of ice cream.

Cover with more whipped cream and top with the rocky road. Stick the marshmallow skewers in, top with a scoop of ice cream and decorate with the bubblegum balls.

PEPPERMINT PILE-UP

SHAKE

4 Peppermint Patties
750 ml (25½ fl oz/3 cups)
  milk
125 ml (4 fl oz/½ cup)
  Chocolate syrup
  (page 120)
½ teaspoon peppermint
  extract
3 scoops vanilla ice cream
1 teaspoon green food
  colouring

MONSTER YOUR SHAKE

60 ml (2 fl oz/¼ cup)
  peppermint syrup
Choc-mint ganache
  (page 125)
2 scoops vanilla ice cream
Whipped cream (page 122)
2 Choc-chip waffles
  (page 129)
2 choc-mint wafer rolls
2 Peppermint Patties,
  cut in half
green sprinkles, for
  decorating
green cake sugar,
  for decorating

SERVES 2

This shake is pure peppermint joy!

To make the shake, place the Peppermint Patties and 100 ml (3½ fl oz) of the milk in a saucepan over low heat and stir continuously for 5 minutes or until the Peppermint Patties are soft. Remove from the heat and use a potato masher to break up into small pieces. Add the remaining milk and place in the fridge to chill. Combine with the remaining ingredients in a blender or food processor. Blend until smooth and combined.

Line the inside of each glass with peppermint syrup and smear the ganache around the outer rims. Gently pour in the shake and top with a scoop of ice cream.

Using a piping bag fitted with a star nozzle, pipe a generous amount of whipped cream on top of the shakes. Cover with the waffles then decorate with more whipped cream and the wafer rolls, Peppermint Patties, sprinkles and sugar.

JELLY BEAN SCREAM QUEEN

SHAKE

750 ml (25½ fl oz/3 cups) milk
60 ml (2 fl oz/¼ cup) blue raspberry (blue heaven) syrup
4 scoops vanilla ice cream

MONSTER YOUR SHAKE

Blue raspberry (blue heaven) syrup, for drizzling
Buttercream frosting (page 124)
rainbow sprinkles, for decorating
2 scoops vanilla ice cream
2 Frosted donuts, coloured blue (page 132)
Whipped cream (page 122)
2 large lollipops
jelly beans, for decorating
silver cachous pearls, for decorating

SERVES 2

All the goodness of a big bowl of jelly beans writ large as a shake. Dig in!

To make the shake, combine the ingredients in a blender or food processor. Blend until smooth and combined.

Line the outside of each glass with syrup. Using a spatula, smear the frosting around the outer rims, then decorate with the sprinkles. Gently pour in the shake and top with a scoop of ice cream.

Place a donut on top of the glass. Using a piping bag fitted with a large star nozzle, fill the donut hole with whipped cream. Stick in the lollipop and decorate with the the jelly beans and cachous pearls.

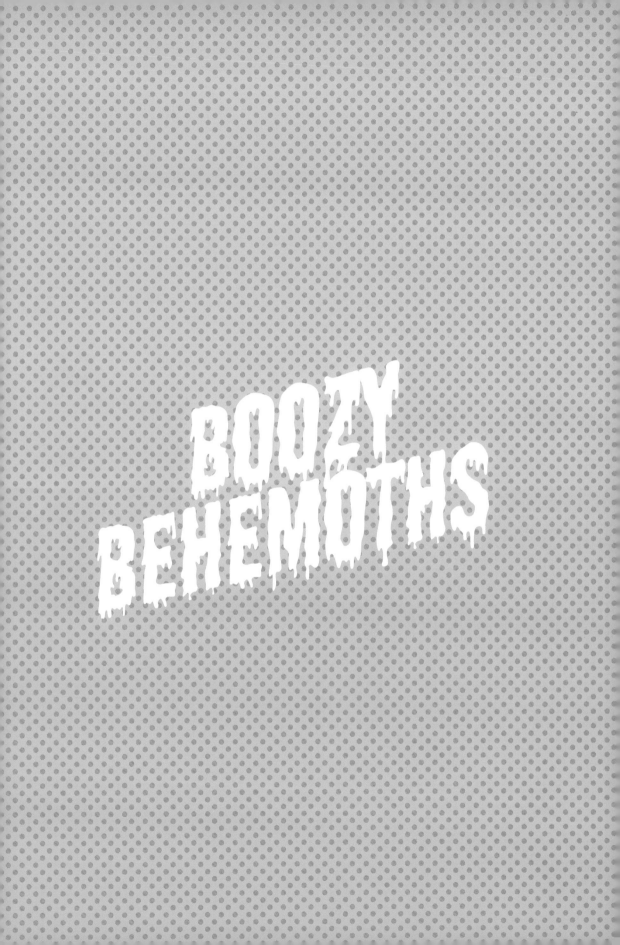

DO YOU LIKE PIÑA COLADAS?

SHAKE

125 ml (4 fl oz/½ cup) milk
125 ml (4 fl oz/½ cup)
 coconut milk
250 ml (8½ fl oz/1 cup)
 coconut cream
250 ml (8½ fl oz/1 cup)
 pineapple juice
100 ml (3½ fl oz) dark rum
2 scoops coconut ice
 cream

MONSTER YOUR SHAKE

30 g (1 oz/½ cup) coconut
 flakes
Whipped cream (page 122)
yellow cake sugar, for
 decorating
2 scoops coconut ice
 cream
1 rice puff (Rice Krispies)
 bar, cut in half on an
 angle
2 lime popsicles
2 wedges fresh pineapple
1 teaspoon lime zest
glacé cherries, for
 decorating

SERVES 2

A wicked tropical delight laced with rum.

Lightly toast the coconut flakes in a small saucepan over low heat for 2 minutes or until lightly browned.

To make the shake, combine the ingredients in a blender or food processor. Blend until smooth and combined.

Using a spatula, smear some of the whipped cream around the outer rim of each glass then decorate with the yellow sugar. Gently pour in the shake and top with a scoop of ice cream. Using a piping bag fitted with a star nozzle, top the shake with a swirl of whipped cream.

Place the rice puff bar pieces onto the glasses and gently insert the popsicles into the shake, filling any gaps with more whipped cream. Decorate with the pineapple, toasted coconut, lime zest, cherries and more yellow sugar.

STRAWBERRY MARGARITA MADNESS

SHAKE

500 ml (17 fl oz/2 cups) coconut water
225 g (8 oz) frozen strawberries
125 ml (4 fl oz/½ cup) Strawberry syrup (page 121)
100 ml (3½ fl oz) tequila
70 ml (2¼ fl oz) Cointreau
1 tablespoon lime juice
2 scoops strawberry sorbet

MONSTER YOUR SHAKE

Strawberry syrup (page 121)
2 scoops strawberry sorbet
Whipped cream (page 122)
2 Strawberry waffles (page 129)
2 strawberry popsicles
1 strawberry sour strap, cut in half
1 strawberry, cut in half

SERVES 2

Sweet strawberry waffles and tequila? Breakfast of champions.

To make the shake, combine the ingredients in a blender or food processor. Blend until smooth and combined.

Line the inside of the glasses with strawberry syrup, reserving a little for topping. Gently pour in the shake and top with a scoop of sorbet. Using a piping bag fitted with a star nozzle, top the shake with a swirl of whipped cream.

Place the waffles on top of the glasses and pipe on more whipped cream. Top with the popsicles and the sour strap and strawberry halves. Drizzle with the remaining syrup.

GOOD JU-JU MINT JULEP

SHAKE

500 ml (17 fl oz/2 cups)
  milk
125 ml (4 fl oz/½ cup)
  bourbon
4 scoops choc-chip ice
  cream
25 g (1 oz/½ cup) mint
  leaves

MONSTER YOUR SHAKE

Choc-mint ganache
  (page 125)
green sprinkles, for
  decorating
4 scoops choc-chip ice
  cream
Whipped cream (page 122)
2 mini ice cream cones
1 large choc-chip cookie,
  cut in half
mint sprigs, for decorating

SERVES 2

Get your southern gothic on with this take on the bourbon-laced classic.

To make the shake, combine the ingredients in a blender or food processor. Blend until smooth and combined.

Smear the inside and outer rims of the glasses with the ganache, then decorate with the green sprinkles. Gently pour in the shake and top with a scoop of ice cream and a big spoonful of whipped cream.

Fill the cones with the remaining ice cream and carefully place upside down on the shake. Stick the cookie pieces in and decorate with mint sprigs.

STRAWBERRY DAIQUIRI! KILL! KILL!

SHAKE

300 g (10½ oz/2 cups)
  frozen strawberries
125 ml (4 fl oz/½ cup)
  Strawberry syrup
  (page 121)
250 ml (8½ fl oz/1 cup)
  light rum
2 tablespoons lime juice
2 tablespoons agave syrup
4 scoops strawberry sorbet

MONSTER YOUR SHAKE

White chocolate ganache
  (page 125)
Strawberry syrup (page 121)
2 scoops strawberry sorbet
Whipped cream (page 122)
2 fresh strawberries,
  cut in half
pink cotton candy, for
  decorating

SERVES 2

Go-go crazy with this refreshing fruity shake – perfect for hot spooky nights.

To make the shake, combine the ingredients in a blender or food processor. Blend until smooth and combined.

Dip the rims of the glasses into the ganache and sit upright, allowing the ganache to drizzle down the glasses. Line the insides with strawberry syrup, then gently pour in the shake and top with a scoop of sorbet. Using a piping bag fitted with a star nozzle, top the shake with a swirl of whipped cream.

Decorate with the strawberries and cotton candy.

IRISH COFFEE CUPCAKE MOUNTAIN

SHAKE

750 ml (25½ fl oz/3 cups) milk
80 ml (2½ fl oz/⅓ cup) Irish cream liqueur (such as Baileys)
80 ml (2½ fl oz/⅓ cup) coffee liqueur (such as Kahlua)
2 scoops vanilla ice cream
1 scoop coffee ice cream

MONSTER YOUR SHAKE

175 g (6 oz/1 cup) dark chocolate buttons
2 scoops coffee ice cream
Coffee whipped cream (page 122)
2 Choc-chip cupcakes (page 131)
mini chocolate candies, for decorating
chocolate sprinkles, for decorating

SERVES 2

Coffee, cream and caramel combine for the ultimate boozy shake.

Place the chocolate buttons in a heatproof bowl set over a saucepan of gently simmering water, making sure the base of the bowl doesn't touch the water. Stir occasionally until melted and smooth. Dip the rims of the glasses into the melted chocolate and sit upright, allowing the chocolate to drizzle down the glasses.

To make the shake, combine the ingredients in a blender or food processor. Blend until smooth and combined.

Gently pour the shake into the glasses and top with a scoop of ice cream. Using a piping bag fitted with a medium round nozzle, pipe whipped cream around the rims of the glasses and on top of the shake.

Top with the cupcakes, pipe on more whipped cream and decorate with the chocolate candies and sprinkles.

SWEET AS A SOUTHERN PEACH

SHAKE

650 ml (22 fl oz) milk
150 ml (5 fl oz) peach iced
    tea syrup
125 ml (4 fl oz/½ cup)
    Southern Comfort
45 g (1½ oz/¼ cup) soft
    brown sugar
3 scoops vanilla ice cream

MONSTER YOUR SHAKE

175 g (6 oz/1 cup) white
    chocolate buttons
pink pearl dust, for
    decorating
Strawberry syrup (page 121)
2 scoops vanilla ice cream
Vanilla bean whipped
    cream (page 122)
2 Cinnamon donuts
    (page 132)
2 mini ice cream waffle
    cones
1 dried peach half, cut
    into quarters
orange and yellow cake
    sugar, for decorating

SERVES 2

Peach iced tea and Southern Comfort are a perfect match.

Place the chocolate buttons in a heatproof bowl set over a saucepan of gently simmering water, making sure the base of the bowl doesn't touch the water. Stir occasionally until melted and smooth. Dip the rims of the glasses into the melted chocolate and sit upright, allowing the chocolate to drizzle down the glasses. Decorate with the pearl dust.

To make the shake, combine the ingredients in a blender or food processor. Blend until smooth and combined.

Line the inside of each glass with strawberry syrup. Gently pour the shake into the glasses and top with a scoop of ice cream. Using a piping bag fitted with a star nozzle, top the shake with a swirl of vanilla whipped cream.

Set the donuts, ice cream cones and dried peach into the cream. Fill the cone with a swirl of cream and decorate with the cake sugar.

KOOKY COCONUT RUM HORCHATA

SHAKE

650 ml (22 fl oz) rice milk
125 ml (4 fl oz/½ cup)
  coconut cream
1 teaspoon ground
  cinnamon
150 ml (5 fl oz) spiced rum
2 tablespoons agave
  nectar
3 scoops vanilla ice cream

MONSTER YOUR SHAKE

30 g (1 oz/½ cup) coconut
  flakes
Whipped coconut cream
  (page 123)
2 scoops vanilla ice cream
Whipped cream (page 122)
2 chocolate-covered
  coconut bars (such as
  Bounty bars), cut into
  different-shaped pieces
2 Whipped cream-filled
  donuts (page 132)

SERVES 2

Celebrate the Day of the Dead with this Mexican-inspired shake.

Lightly toast the coconut flakes in a small saucepan over low heat for 2 minutes or until lightly browned. Set aside.

To make the shake, combine the ingredients in a blender or food processor. Blend until smooth and combined.

Using a spatula, smear some of the whipped coconut cream around the outer rim of each glass then sprinkle with some of the toasted coconut flakes. Smear a little more of the coconut cream on the inside of the glasses. Gently pour in the shake and top with a scoop of ice cream. Using a piping bag fitted with a large star nozzle, top the shake with a large swirl of whipped cream.

Thread a few pieces of the coconut bars onto two skewers. Place the donuts on top of the shake, and decorate with more whipped cream, the coconut bar pieces and skewers, and the remaining toasted coconut.

CHOC-CHIP COOKIE BROWNIE BEAST

SHAKE

500 ml (17 fl oz/2 cups)
  milk
250 ml (8½ fl oz/1 cup) Irish
  cream liqueur (such as
  Baileys)
3 choc-chip cookies
2 scoops choc-chip
  ice cream

MONSTER YOUR SHAKE

Chocolate syrup (page 120)
2 scoops choc-chip ice
  cream
Whipped cream (page 122)
2 Chocolate brownies
  (page 130)
6 choc-chip cookies

SERVES 2

A terrifyingly grown-up take on milk and cookies.

To make the shake, combine the ingredients in a blender or food processor. Blend until smooth and combined.

Line the inside of the glasses with chocolate syrup. Gently pour in the shake and top with a scoop of ice cream. Using a piping bag fitted with a star nozzle, top the shake with a generous amount of whipped cream.

Place the brownies on top of the shakes, then top with a stack of cookies, piping whipped cream between each.

COFFEE CHOCOLATE COOKIE CATACLYSM

SHAKE

625 ml (21 fl oz/2½ cups)
  milk
150 ml (5 fl oz) coffee
  liqueur (such as Kahlua)
4 Oreo cookies
3 scoops chocolate ice
  cream

MONSTER YOUR SHAKE

Chocolate syrup (page 120)
Coffee whipped cream
  (page 122)
6 Mini Oreo cookies,
  roughly chopped
½ Flake chocolate bar,
  roughly chopped
2 scoops coffee ice cream
Whipped cream (page 122)
2 Chocolate ganache-filled
  donuts (page 132)
8 Oreo cookies

SERVES 2

A disastrously delicious coffee crunch.

To make the shake, combine the ingredients in a blender or food processor. Blend until smooth and combined.

Line the inside of each glass with most of the chocolate syrup. Using a spatula, smear some of the coffee whipped cream around the outer rim of each glass then sprinkle with the chopped mini Oreos and most of the chopped Flake. Gently pour in the shake and top with a scoop of ice cream. Using a piping bag fitted with a star nozzle, cover the shakes with a generous amount of whipped cream.

Set the donuts and one Oreo cookie on top, then stack the remaining cookies, piping whipped cream between each. Drizzle with the remaining chocolate syrup and sprinkle with the remaining Flake.

NUTTY ALMOND FREAK OUT

SHAKE

625 ml (21 fl oz/2½ cups)
  milk
125 ml (4 fl oz/½ cup)
  almond liqueur (such
  as Amaretto)
4 scoops vanilla ice cream

MONSTER YOUR SHAKE

Whipped cream (page 122)
2 tablespoons chopped
  almonds
2 scoops vanilla ice cream
8 pieces thin almond
  biscotti
3 choc-covered almonds,
  chopped

SERVES 2

The perfect shake for anyone who's crazy about almonds.

To make the shake, combine the ingredients in a blender or food processor. Blend until smooth and combined.

Using a spatula, smear some of the whipped cream around the outer rim of each glass then sprinkle with the chopped almonds. Gently pour in the shake and top with a scoop of ice cream.

Spoon on more whipped cream and top with a piece of biscotti. Repeat with another two layers of biscotti and ice cream. Roughly break up the remaining two pieces of biscotti and place on top of the shake along with the chopped chocolate almonds.

DEATH BY DESSERT

BIG BANG BIRTHDAY CAKE

SHAKE

625 ml (21 fl oz/2½ cups)
  milk
150 g (5½ oz/1 cup) vanilla
  instant cake mix
4 scoops vanilla ice cream

MONSTER YOUR SHAKE

Buttercream frosting
  (page 124)
rainbow sprinkles, for
  decorating
2 scoops vanilla ice cream
Vanilla bean whipped
  cream (page 122)
2 Mini confetti cupcakes
  (page 131)
coloured popcorn,
  for decorating
cotton candy, for
  decorating

SERVES 2

What better time for rainbow-coloured excess than a birthday?

To make the shake, combine the ingredients in a blender or food processor. Blend until smooth and combined.

Using a spatula, smear the frosting around the outer rim of each glass then decorate with the sprinkles. Gently pour in the shake and top with a scoop of ice cream.

Using a piping bag fitted with a star nozzle, cover the shakes with a generous swirl of whipped cream.

Push the cupcakes onto skewers and stick into the shake. Pile with a mound of coloured popcorn and decorate with cotton candy.

RED VELVET REVENGE

SHAKE

625 ml (21 fl oz/2½ cups) milk
150 g (5½ oz/1 cup) red velvet instant cake mix
4 scoops chocolate ice cream

MONSTER YOUR SHAKE

Raspberry syrup (page 121)
Cream cheese frosting (page 125)
red sprinkles and red glitter sparkles, for decorating
2 scoops chocolate ice cream
2 cherry–coconut bars (such as Cherry Ripe), cut into pieces
2 Red velvet cupcakes (page 131)
Whipped cream (page 122)

SERVES 2

This shake will have you seeing red – sweet, sweet red.

To make the shake, combine the ingredients in a blender or food processor. Blend until smooth and combined.

Line the inside of each glass with raspberry syrup. Using a spatula, smear the frosting around the outer rims, then decorate with the sprinkles and glitter. Gently pour in the shake and top with a scoop of ice cream.

Set a piece of Cherry Ripe across the top of each glass followed by a cupcake.

Using a piping bag fitted with a star nozzle, pipe whipped cream into any gaps on top of the shake. Decorate with the remaining pieces of Cherry Ripe and with more sprinkles.

PUMPKINHEAD PIE

SHAKE

200 g (7 oz) diced pumpkin
750 ml (25½ fl oz/3 cups)
  milk
3 tablespoons maple syrup
2 teaspoons ground
  cinnamon
pinch of ground allspice
pinch of ground nutmeg
½ teaspoon vanilla essence
2 scoops vanilla ice cream

MONSTER YOUR SHAKE

Buttercream frosting
  (page 124)
2 scoops vanilla ice cream
Vanilla bean whipped
  cream (page 122)
Caramel syrup (page 120)
2 Cinnamon donuts
  (page 132)
2 vanilla macarons
ground cinnamon, for
  dusting

SERVES 2

Like a taste of Halloween – this shake is frighteningly good.

To make the shake, place the pumpkin in a small saucepan and cover with water. Cook over a medium heat for 8 minutes or until soft. Drain and return to the saucepan. Using a hand-held blender, puree the pumpkin until smooth. Set aside to cool. Combine with the remaining ingredients in a blender or food processor and blend until smooth and combined.

Using a spatula, smear the frosting around the outer rim of each glass. Gently pour in the shake and top with a scoop of ice cream. Using a piping bag fitted with a star nozzle, top with swirls of whipped cream.

Drizzle the outside of the glasses with caramel syrup and top with the donuts, macarons and a dusting of cinnamon.

FUDGE BROWNIE CHOC SLUDGE

SHAKE

625 ml (21 fl oz/2½ cups)
  milk
125 ml (4 fl oz/½ cup)
  Chocolate syrup
  (page 120)
5 scoops chocolate fudge
  ice cream

MONSTER YOUR SHAKE

Chocolate ganache
  (page 125)
Whipped cream (page 122)
10 pretzels
4 scoops chocolate fudge
  ice cream
2 Chocolate brownies
  (page 130)
chopped Malteasers,
  for decorating

SERVES 2

A choc-fudge brownie beast.

To make the shake, combine the ingredients in
a blender or food processor. Blend until smooth
and combined.

Smear chocolate ganache on the inside of
each glass, reserving a little for topping. Using
a spatula, smear some of the whipped cream
around the outer rims, then decorate with the
pretzels. Gently pour in the shake and top with
a scoop of ice cream.

Spoon more whipped cream on top of the
shakes and place a chocolate brownie on top of
each glass. Cover with whipped cream, a scoop
of ice cream and more ganache. Sprinkle with
the chopped Malteasers.

JELLY DONUT BLOODY MURDER

SHAKE

625 ml (21 fl oz/2½ cups) milk
250 ml (8½ fl oz/1 cup) Raspberry syrup (page 121)
125 g (4½ oz/1 cup) fresh or frozen raspberries
1 teaspoon ground cinnamon
2 scoops vanilla ice cream

MONSTER YOUR SHAKE

Raspberry syrup (page 121)
2 scoops vanilla ice cream
Whipped cream (page 122)
2 Jelly/jam-filled donuts (page 132)
6 mini raspberry Kit Kats, broken into fingers
pink and red sprinkles, for decorating

SERVES 2

Oozing with raspberry syrup, this shake will have you screaming for more.

To make the shake, combine the ingredients in a blender or food processor. Blend until smooth and combined.

Fill two food-safe plastic syringes with raspberry syrup and set aside.

Line the inside of each glass with raspberry syrup. Gently pour in the shake and top with a scoop of ice cream. Using a piping bag fitted with a star nozzle, cover the shakes with whipped cream.

Place the donuts on top of the cream, stick in the syringes and decorate with the Kit Kats and sprinkles.

LEMON MERINGUE MASSACRE

SHAKE

625 ml (21 fl oz/2½ cups)
    milk
315 g (11 oz/1 cup) Lemon
    curd (page 126)
2 tablespoons fresh lemon
    juice
1 tablespoon lemon zest
2 scoops vanilla ice cream

MONSTER YOUR SHAKE

Lemon buttercream
    frosting (page 124)
2 scoops vanilla ice cream
2 butter–coconut cookies
    (such as Butternut Snaps)
Italian meringue topping
    (page 123)
Lemon curd (page 126)
½ tablespoon lemon zest
2 candied lemon slices
vanilla cotton candy,
    for decorating

SERVES 2

A tangy lemon treat that will put a smile on even the sourest of dials.

To make the shake, combine the ingredients in a blender or food processor. Blend until smooth and combined.

Using a spatula, smear the frosting on the inside and around the outer rim of each glass. Gently pour in the shake and top with a scoop of ice cream.

Place the cookies on top of the glasses and, using a piping bag fitted with a large round nozzle, cover with swirls of meringue. Lightly brown using a kitchen blowtorch then decorate with lemon curd, lemon zest, candied lemon and cotton candy.

MAPLE-PECAN TOWER OF TERROR

SHAKE

750 ml (25½ fl oz/3 cups)
  milk
60 ml (2 fl oz/¼ cup)
  Caramel syrup (page 120)
60 ml (2 fl oz/¼ cup) maple
  syrup
4 scoops pecan ice cream

MONSTER YOUR SHAKE

2 scoops pecan ice cream
Whipped cream (page 122)
8 Mini pecan hotcakes
  (page 129)
1 tablespoon chopped
  pecans
maple syrup, for drizzling

SERVES 2

Reach dizzying new heights of deliciousness with this hotcake-topped wonder.

To make the shake, combine the ingredients in a blender or food processor. Blend until smooth and combined.

Pour the shake into the glasses and top with a scoop of ice cream. Using a piping bag fitted with a star nozzle, top the shakes and rims of the glasses with whipped cream. Cover with a hotcake and a swirl of whipped cream. Repeat with the remaining hotcakes.

Carefully top with the remaining ice cream, scatter with the pecans and drizzle with maple syrup.

SCARY CAMPFIRE S'MORES

SHAKE

750 ml (25½ fl oz/3 cups)
   milk
1 cup marshmallow creme
   (such as Marshmallow Fluff)
125 ml (4 fl oz/½ cup)
   Chocolate syrup
   (page 120)
5 scoops vanilla ice cream

MONSTER YOUR SHAKE

225 g (8 oz) chopped milk
   chocolate
2 scoops vanilla ice cream
marshmallow creme (such
   as Marshmallow Fluff),
   for decorating
4 large marshmallows
4 graham crackers

SERVES 2

A campfire classic in your own kitchen.

Place the chopped chocolate in a heatproof bowl set over a saucepan of gently simmering water, making sure the base of the bowl doesn't touch the water. Stir occasionally until the chocolate is melted and smooth.

To make the shake, combine the ingredients in a blender or food processor. Blend until smooth and combined.

Line the inside of each glass with some of the melted chocolate. Gently pour in the shake and top with a scoop of ice cream. Using a spatula, smear the marshmallow fluff around the outer rim of each glass.

Place the marshmallows on a baking tray and lightly brown using a kitchen blowtorch.

Place a graham cracker onto each glass, spoon on some melted chocolate and top with a marshmallow. Repeat.

BANOFFEE BROUHAHA

SHAKE

625 ml (21 fl oz/2½ cups)
  milk
60 ml (2 fl oz/¼ cup)
  Caramel syrup (page 120)
2 bananas
160 g (6 oz/½ cup)
  sweetened condensed
  milk
4 scoops vanilla ice cream

MONSTER YOUR SHAKE

Buttercream frosting
  (page 124)
60 g (2 oz/¼ cup) chopped
  walnuts
2 scoops vanilla ice cream
Whipped cream (page 122)
6 choc–banana Pocky sticks
Chocolate popcorn
  (page 127)
choc–caramel chips, for
  decorating
Caramel syrup (page 120)

SERVES 2

This chocolate, banana and caramel shake is gauranteed to turn you into a drooling mess.

To make the shake, combine the ingredients in a blender or food processor. Blend until smooth and combined.

Using a spatula, smear the frosting around the outer rim of each glass then sprinkle with the chopped walnuts. Gently pour in the shake and top with a scoop of ice cream. Using a piping bag fitted with a star nozzle, cover the shakes with swirls of whipped cream.

Stick the Pocky sticks into the shake and pile on the chocolate popcorn. Decorate with the choc–caramel chips and drizzle with caramel syrup.

KEY LIME PIE IN THE SKY

SHAKE

375 ml (12½ fl oz/1½ cups)
  milk
375 ml (12½ fl oz/1½ cups)
  coconut milk
200 g (7 oz) Lime curd
  (page 126)
2 tablespoons fresh
  lime juice
2 tablespoon lime zest
2 scoops vanilla ice cream

MONSTER YOUR SHAKE

1 marshmallow, cut in half
Lime curd (page 126)
Vanilla bean whipped
  cream (page 122)
2 scoops vanilla ice cream
8 ginger nut (ginger snap)
  cookies
1 tablespoon lime zest
sweetened condensed
  milk, for drizzling

SERVES 2

Sweet and sour come together like magic in this heavenly concoction.

To make the shake, combine the ingredients in a blender or food processor. Blend until smooth and combined.

Place the marshmallow halves on a baking tray and lightly brown using a kitchen blowtorch.

Line the inside of each glass with some of the lime curd. Using a spatula, smear some of the whipped cream around the outer rims. Gently pour in the shake and top with a scoop of ice cream.

In a small bowl place a few tablespoons each of the whipped cream and lime curd. Lightly fold together to create a marbled effect. Spoon a small amount on top of the shakes and cover with a cookie. Repeat with the remaining cookies. Top with the toasted marshmallow and lime zest, and drizzle with sweetened condensed milk.

BASICS

CHOCOLATE SYRUP

MAKES 500 ML (17 FL OZ/2 CUPS)

110 g (4 oz/½ cup) sugar
125 ml (4 fl oz/½ cup) light corn syrup
90 g (3 oz/¾ cup) cocoa powder
100 g (3½ oz) dark chocolate buttons

Combine the sugar, corn syrup and cocoa powder with 250 ml (8½ fl oz/1 cup) water in a medium-sized saucepan over low heat. Stir for 2 minutes until the sugar has dissolved.

Remove from the heat and add the chocolate buttons, stirring for 3 minutes or until melted.

Set aside to cool completely before transferring into a squeeze bottle or container.

The syrup will keep in the fridge for up to 1 week.

CARAMEL SYRUP

MAKES 500 ML (17 FL OZ/2 CUPS)

330 g (11½ oz/1½ cups) sugar
125 g (4½ oz/⅔ cup lightly packed) brown sugar
300 ml (10 fl oz) thickened cream

Combine the sugar with 60 ml (2 fl oz/¼ cup) water in a medium-sized saucepan over low heat. Stir constantly for 2 minutes until the sugar has dissolved, brushing any sugar from the side of the pan with a wet pastry brush. Increase the heat to medium–high and boil for 2 minutes then reduce the heat to medium and simmer without stirring for 10 minutes or until golden.

Remove from the heat and add the brown sugar and cream and stir until combined. Return to medium heat and stir for 2 minutes until smooth. Do not boil.

Set aside to cool completely before transferring into a squeeze bottle or container.

The syrup will keep in the fridge for up to 2 weeks.

VARIATION

For **Salted caramel syrup**, add 1 tablespoon of salt when adding the brown sugar and cream.

RASPBERRY SYRUP

MAKES 500 ML (17 FL OZ/2 CUPS)

55 g (2 oz/¼ cup) caster (superfine) sugar
250 g (9 oz) fresh or frozen raspberries
150 g (5½ oz/½ cup) raspberry jam
1½ tablespoons glucose syrup

Combine the sugar with
1½ tablespoons water in a medium-sized saucepan over low heat. Stir constantly for 2 minutes until the sugar has dissolved, brushing any sugar from the side of the pan with a wet pastry brush. Add the remaining ingredients and stir for 1 minute or until well combined.

Remove from the heat and set aside to cool completely. Puree with a hand-held blender for 1 minute or until smooth. Transfer into a squeeze bottle or container.

The syrup will keep in the fridge for up to 1 week.

NOTE

For a smooth syrup, pass the pureed mixture through a fine-mesh sieve.

STRAWBERRY SYRUP

MAKES 500 ML (17 FL OZ/2 CUPS)

1½ tablespoons caster (superfine) sugar
250 g (9 oz) strawberries, hulled
150g (5½ oz/½ cup) strawberry jam
1½ tablespoons glucose syrup

Combine the sugar with
1½ tablespoons water in a medium-sized saucepan over low heat. Stir constantly for 2 minutes until the sugar has dissolved, brushing any sugar from the side of the pan with a wet pastry brush. Add the remaining ingredients and stir for 1 minute or until well combined.

Remove from the heat and set aside to cool completely. Puree with a hand-held blender for 1 minute or until smooth. Transfer into a squeeze bottle or container.

The syrup will keep in the fridge for up to 1 week.

WHIPPED CREAM

MAKES 625 ML (21 FL OZ/2½ CUPS)

300 ml (10 fl oz) thickened cream

Place the cream in a medium-sized bowl along with any ingredients for variations, if using. Using an electric mixer, beat on medium speed for 3–4 minutes until the cream is fluffy and holds soft peaks.

Use immediately or transfer to an airtight container. The whipped cream will keep in the fridge for up to 1 week.

VARIATIONS

To colour whipped cream, add 1 drop food colouring and keep adding drops as you beat until you reach your desired shade.

For **Coffee whipped cream**, add 1 tablespoon instant coffee granules and 3 tablespoons icing (confectioners') sugar.

For **Peppermint whipped cream**, add 5 drops peppermint essence and 2 tablespoons icing (confectioners') sugar.

For **Strawberry whipped cream**, add 5 drops strawberry essence and 2 tablespoons icing (confectioners') sugar.

For **Vanilla bean whipped cream**, add 1 teaspoon vanilla bean paste and 2 tablespoons icing (confectioners') sugar.

For **Orange blossom whipped cream**, add 2 tablespoons orange blossom water, 1 teaspoon orange zest and 2 tablespoons icing (confectioners') sugar.

For **Rose whipped cream**, add 2 tablespoons rose water, 2 tablespoons icing (confectioners') sugar and 1 drop red food colouring.

WHIPPED COCONUT CREAM

MAKES 250 ML (8½ FL OZ/1 CUP)

2 x 400 ml (13½ fl oz) tins full-fat coconut milk, refrigerated overnight
1 tablespoon maple syrup
1 tablespoon vanilla extract

Carefully scoop the solidified part of the refrigerated coconut milk from the tins into a large mixing bowl. Discard the watery contents at the bottom of the tins or reserve for another use. Add the maple syrup and vanilla to the bowl. Using an electric mixer, beat on medium speed for 3–4 minutes until the cream is fluffy and holds soft peaks.

Use immediately or transfer to an airtight container. The whipped coconut cream will keep in the fridge for up to 1 week – beat for 2 minutes or until creamy before using.

ITALIAN MERINGUE TOPPING

MAKES 310 ML (10½ FL OZ/1¼ CUPS)

170 g (6 oz/¾ cup) caster (superfine) sugar
2 egg whites
½ teaspoon cream of tartar

Place the sugar and 60 ml (2 fl oz/¼ cup) water in a medium-sized saucepan over low heat. Stir until the sugar dissolves, increase the heat to high and, measuring with a candy thermometer, cook until the syrup reaches 120°C (250°F). This should take 6–8 minutes.

Meanwhile, place the egg whites and cream of tartar in a bowl and, using an electric mixer, beat on low speed for 5–6 minutes until the cream is fluffy and holds soft peaks. With the beaters running, slowly add the syrup. Increase the speed to medium–high and beat for 5 minutes or until the mixture is thick, glossy and holds stiff peaks. Leave the mixer running on low until ready to use.

BUTTERCREAM FROSTING

**MAKES 375 G
(13 OZ/1½ CUPS)**

125 g (4½ oz/½ cup)
  unsalted butter, softened
185 g (6 ½ oz/1½ cups)
  icing (confectioners')
  sugar, sifted
2 tablespoons milk

Place the butter in a medium-sized bowl. Using an electric mixer, beat on high speed for 5 minutes or until pale and fluffy. Gradually beat in half the icing sugar and the milk, then the remaining icing sugar. Beat for 4 minutes or until the sugar has dissolved and the mixture is smooth.

Add any ingredients for variations into the mixture, if using, and beat for another 1 minute.

Use immediately or transfer to an airtight container. The frosting will keep in the fridge for up to 1 week.

NOTE

If you've pre-made the frosting and stored it in the fridge, allow to sit for 20 minutes at room temperature to soften.

VARIATIONS

To **colour buttercream frosting**, add 1 drop food colouring and keep adding drops as you stir until you reach your desired shade.

For **Chocolate buttercream frosting**, add 1 tablespoon sifted cocoa powder.

For **Mocha buttercream frosting**, add 1 tablespoon instant coffee granules and 1 tablespoon cocoa powder.

For **Lemon buttercream frosting**, add 1 tablespoon lemon juice and 1 tablespoon lemon zest.

For **Choc-mint buttercream frosting** add 1 tablespoon cocoa powder and ¼ teaspoon peppermint essence.

CREAM CHEESE FROSTING

MAKES 250 G (9 OZ/1 CUP)

30 g (1 oz) butter, softened
60 g (2 oz) cream cheese, softened
½ teaspoon vanilla essence
1–2 tablespoons lemon juice
1 teaspoon lemon zest (optional)
125 g (4½ oz/1 cup) icing (confectioners') sugar

Place the butter, cream cheese, vanilla and lemon juice and zest, if using, in a medium-sized bowl. Using an electric mixer, beat on high speed for 4 minutes or until pale and fluffy. Gradually add the icing sugar and beat for 4 minutes or until the sugar has dissolved and the mixture is smooth.

Use immediately or transfer to an airtight container. The frosting will keep in the fridge for up to 1 week.

CHOCOLATE GANACHE

MAKES 310 G (11 OZ/1¼ CUPS)

250 g (9 oz) dark cooking chocolate, broken into pieces
80 ml (2½ fl oz/⅓ cup) thickened cream

Place the chocolate and cream in a heatproof bowl set over a saucepan of gently simmering water, making sure the base of the bowl doesn't touch the water. Stir occasionally for 3–4 minutes until melted and smooth. Add any ingredients for variations into the mixture, if using, and stir until combined.

Set aside to cool for 10–15 minutes, stirring occasionally, until the ganache is nice and thick.

VARIATIONS

For **White chocolate ganache**, replace the dark cooking chocolate with white chocolate.

For **Choc-mint ganache** add ¼ teaspoon peppermint essence.

LEMON CURD

MAKES 500 G (1 LB 2 OZ/2 CUPS)

2 eggs
2 egg yolks
170 g (6 oz/¾ cup) caster (superfine) sugar
90 g (3 oz/⅓ cup) chilled unsalted butter,
  chopped
zest and juice of 2 lemons

In a medium-sized saucepan, whisk the eggs, yolks and caster sugar for 4 minutes or until smooth and pale. Place over low heat and add the butter, lemon zest and juice, and whisk the mixture constantly for 3–4 minutes or until thickened.

Remove from the heat and allow to cool for 30 minutes. If you prefer a totally smooth curd without zest, pass through a fine-mesh sieve.

The curd will keep in an airtight container in the fridge for up to 1 week.

VARIATIONS

For **Lime curd**, substitute the lemon for the zest and juice of 2 limes.

For **Orange curd**, substitute the lemon for the zest and juice of 1 orange.

For **Passionfruit curd**, substitute the lemon for 90 g (3 oz/⅓ cup) passionfruit pulp.

CHOC-DIPPED ORANGES

MAKES 20 PIECES

1 orange, halved and cut into thin slices
175 g (6 oz) dark chocolate buttons

Preheat the oven to 70°C (160°F).

Place the orange slices on a wire rack set over a baking tray and place in the oven for 3 hours or until dehydrated.

Meanwhile, place the chocolate buttons in a heatproof bowl set over a saucepan of gently simmering water, making sure the base of the bowl doesn't touch the water. Stir occasionally until melted and smooth, then set aside to cool slightly.

Dip each orange slice half way into the melted chocolate and place back on the wire rack to set.

The choc-dipped oranges will keep in an airtight container for up to 1 month.

BUTTERSCOTCH POPCORN

MAKES ABOUT 3 CUPS

2 tablespoons vegetable oil
50 g (1¾ oz/¼ cup) popping corn kernels
½ teaspoon salt
110 g (4 oz/½ cup) sugar
125 g (4½ oz/½ cup) chilled unsalted
  butter, cubed

Heat the oil in a large saucepan over medium heat. Add the corn, cover with a lid and cook, shaking the pan occasionally, until the corn has finished popping. Remove from the heat, add the salt and set aside to cool.

Meanwhile, place the sugar in a mound in the middle of a small saucepan. Set over medium heat and pour 60 ml (2 fl oz/¼ cup) water around the sugar. Without stirring, bring to a simmer. Reduce the heat to low and allow to cook for 4–5 minutes or until the mixture turns a rich amber colour and any foam disappears. Add the butter, one cube at a time, whisking for 2–3 minutes until thick.

Remove from the heat. Set some of the sauce aside for your shake and pour the remainder over the popcorn, stirring with a large spoon to coat thoroughly. Turn out onto a baking paper-lined tray and allow to set. Break into bite-sized pieces.

CHOCOLATE POPCORN

MAKES ABOUT 3 CUPS

2 tablespoons vegetable oil
50 g (1¾ oz/¼ cup) popping corn kernels
175 g (1 cup) dark chocolate buttons

Heat the oil in a large saucepan over medium heat. Add the corn, cover with a lid and cook, shaking the pan occasionally, until the corn has finished popping. Remove from the heat and set aside to cool.

Meanwhile, place the chocolate buttons in a heatproof bowl set over a saucepan of gently simmering water, making sure the base of the bowl doesn't touch the water. Stir occasionally until melted and smooth, then set aside to cool slightly.

Pour the melted chocolate over the popcorn, stirring with a large spoon to coat thoroughly. Turn out onto a baking paper-lined tray and allow to set. Break into bite-sized pieces.

CANDIED BACON

MAKES 4 SLICES

4 slices streaky bacon
maple syrup, for brushing

Preheat the oven to 180°C (350°F).

Place the bacon on a baking paper-lined baking tray and place in the oven for 10 minutes or until the bacon is browned.

Brush the bacon liberally with maple syrup and return to the oven for 5 minutes until crisp. Transfer to a wire rack to cool.

FRENCH TOAST

MAKES 2 SLICES

1 egg
60 ml (2 fl oz/¼ cup) milk
2 slices sourdough bread

Beat the eggs and milk together in a shallow dish then dip each slice of bread into the mixture, soaking both sides well.

Heat a non-stick frying pan over medium heat and fry the bread for 2 minutes on each side until golden. Set aside to cool slightly before using.

MINI PECAN HOTCAKES

MAKES 8–10

150 g (5½ oz/1 cup) self-raising flour
2 tablespoons caster (superfine) sugar
½ teaspoon ground cinnamon
30 g (1 oz/¼ cup) chopped pecans
185 ml (6 fl oz/¾ cup) milk
1 egg

Sift the flour, sugar and cinnamon into a medium-sized mixing bowl and add the pecans.

In a separate bowl, whisk together the milk and egg. Add to the dry ingredients and continue to whisk for 1 minute or until well incorporated.

Spray a medium-sized frying pan with vegetable oil spray and heat over low–medium heat. Pour in the batter in 2 tablespoon amounts and cook until bubbles appear on the surface. Flip and cook for another minute until golden. Set aside on a plate to cool.

WAFFLES

MAKES 4 LARGE WAFFLES

150 g (5½ oz/1 cup) self-raising flour
1 tablespoon sugar
185 ml (6 fl oz/¾ cup) milk
3 tablespoons vegetable oil
1 egg

Preheat a waffle maker to medium–high. Grease if necessary.

Combine the flour and sugar in a medium-sized mixing bowl. In a separate bowl, whisk together the milk, oil and egg.

Slowly pour the wet mixture into the dry ingredients, and add any ingredients for variations, if using. Mix well (but it's okay to have a few lumpy bits here and there).

Pour 60 ml (2 fl oz/¼ cup) amounts of batter into the waffle maker and cook each one for 3–4 minutes until golden brown. Carefully remove and set aside to cool.

VARIATIONS

For **Choc-chip waffles**, add 90 g (3 oz/¾ cup) white, dark or milk choc chips

For **Berry waffles**, add 100 g (3½ oz) frozen berries of your choice. Be sure to add the berries straight from the freezer. Partially defrosted fruit will result in a very soggy waffle!

CHOCOLATE BROWNIES

MAKES 9–12 BROWNIES

180 g (6½ oz) butter
250 g (9 oz) dark cooking
  chocolate, broken into
  pieces
3 eggs
330 g (11½ oz/1½ cups)
  sugar
2 teaspoons vanilla extract
150 g (5½ oz/1 cup) plain
  (all-purpose) flour
60 g (2 oz/½ cup) cocoa
  powder
150 g (5½ oz/1 cup)
  chocolate buttons

Preheat the oven to 180°C (350°F). Grease and line a 20 cm (8 in) square baking tin with baking paper.

Place the butter in a medium-sized saucepan over low heat for 2 minutes or until melted. Remove from the heat, add the chocolate and stir until melted. Set aside to cool.

Meanwhile, place the eggs, sugar and vanilla in a bowl and, using an electric mixer, beat on medium speed for 5–6 minutes until thick and pale.

Sift the flour and cocoa powder together. Fold into the egg mixture along with the melted chocolate mixture using a large wooden spoon. Gently stir in the chocolate buttons. Pour the batter into the prepared tin and bake for 30–35 minutes.

Allow to cool in the tin before cutting the brownie into squares.

CUPCAKES

**MAKES 12 STANDARD OR
25–30 MINI CUPCAKES**

185 ml (6 fl oz/¾ cup)
   buttermilk
1 egg
125 ml (4 fl oz/½ cup)
   vegetable oil
220 g (8 oz/1½ cups) plain
   (all-purpose) flour
145 g (5 oz/⅔ cup) caster
   (superfine) sugar

Preheat the oven to 180°C (350°F). Lightly grease a 12-hole muffin tin or a 25–30-hole mini-muffin pan, or line with cupcake cases.

Combine the buttermilk, egg and oil in a jug and set aside.

Sift the flour into a large mixing bowl and add the caster sugar. Make a well in the centre and pour in the milk mixture, stirring until just combined. Fold in any ingredients for variations, if using.

Spoon the batter into the muffin holes, filling each to about two-thirds full.

Bake for 20 minutes for regular-sized cupcakes or 8–10 minutes for mini, or until a skewer inserted into the centre comes out clean.

Cool in the pan for 2 minutes before turning out onto a wire rack to cool completely.

VARIATIONS

For **Choc-chip cupcakes**, add 90 g (3 oz/½ cup) white, dark or milk choc chips.

For **Mini confetti cupcakes**, top the cooled mini cupcakes with Buttercream frosting (page 124) and decorate with rainbow sprinkles.

For **Red velvet cupcakes**, add ½ teaspoon sifted cocoa powder, 1 tablespoon red food colouring and ½ teaspoon vanilla essence. Top the cooled cupcakes with Cream cheese frosting (page 125) and decorate with a raspberry.

For **Mini chocolate-topped cupcakes**, top the cooled mini cupcakes with Chocolate ganache (page 125) and decorate with rainbow sprinkles.

DONUTS

MAKES 10–12

250 g (9 oz/1⅔ cup) plain
  (all-purpose) flour
3 tablespoons caster
  (superfine) sugar
2½ teaspoons active
  dried yeast
2 eggs
80 ml (2½ fl oz/⅓ cup)
  warm water
70 g (2½ oz) softened
  unsalted butter, cut into
  9 cubes
vegetable oil for deep-
  frying

Place the flour, sugar, yeast, eggs and water in the bowl of an electric mixer. Mix on low speed for 3 minutes or until combined and elastic. With the motor running, add the butter, one cube at a time, until incorporated. Transfer to a lightly oiled bowl, cover with plastic wrap and set aside in a warm place for 1 hour, or until doubled in size.

Knock back the dough and turn out onto a lightly floured bench. Roll the dough out to 1 cm (½ in). Cut into rounds using an 8 cm (3¼ in) cookie cutter. Use a 2.5 cm (1 in) cutter to cut the holes, if required. Transfer to a lightly oiled baking tray and cover with plastic wrap. Set aside in a warm place for 30 minutes, or until doubled in size.

Heat the oil in a deep-fryer or saucepan to 160°C (320°F). Fry the donuts, in batches, for 1 minute on each side or until golden. Remove with a slotted spoon and drain on paper towel.

VARIATIONS

For **Cinnamon donuts**, combine ½ teaspoon ground cinnamon with 110 g (4 oz/½ cup) sugar and roll still-warm donuts in the mixture.

For **Filled donuts**, place 1 cup of your filling of choice into a piping bag fitted with a 5 mm (¼ in) nozzle. Insert the tip into the side of the donut and squeeze in your desired amount. If you like, roll the filled donuts in sugar or cinnamon sugar.

For **Chocolate-frosted donuts**, dip cooled donuts into warm Chocolate ganache (page 125) followed by chocolate sprinkles. Place on a wire rack to set.

For **Frosted donuts**, combine 125 g (4½ oz/1 cup) icing (confectioners') sugar with 1½ tablespoons water. While mixing, slowly add food colouring until you reach the shade you want. Dip cooled donuts into the frosting followed by sprinkles (if using). Place on a wire rack to set.

AUTHOR THANKS

A heartfelt thank-you to the wonderful Paul McNally for the opportunity to write and style my own title. Its been such an amazing experience and a dream fulfilled. And thank you to the ever so lovely Hannah Koelmeyer and Lucy Heaver for your fantastic editing and patience. My colleague and friend Chris Middleton, thank you for your talented eye and photographic skills in helping me create such beautiful images. Meryl Batlle – my right-hand woman! Your non-stop hard work, gusto and efforts on set each and every day was incredible. You are a true gem. My wonderful partner in life, David – none of this would have been possible without your unwavering support and encouragement. Thank you to you and our Penny and Willy D for putting up with weeks on end of writing, testing and turning our home upside-down! I love you. And last but not least, thank you to my incredible parents Margaret and Peter for instilling a love of food in me from an early age, always being in my corner and encouraging me to pursue this incredibly challenging and fulfilling career path. You are the best cheer squad a girl could ask for.

Published in 2016 by Smith Street Books
Melbourne | Australia
smithstreetbooks.com

ISBN: 978-1-925418-20-0

Publisher: Paul McNally
Project editor: Hannah Koelmeyer, Tusk studio
Design concept: Kate Barraclough
Design layout: Heather Menzies, Studio31 Graphics
Food styling: Vicki Valsamis

Printed & bound in China by C&C Offset Printing Co., Ltd.

Book 19
10 9 8 7 6 5 4 3 2 1